CYBERSECURITY EXPERT

Daniel R. Faust

PowerKiDS
press
New York

Published in 2018 by The Rosen Publishing Group, Inc.
29 East 21st Street, New York, NY 10010

First Edition

Editor: Melissa Raé Shofner
Book Design: Rachel Rising

Photo Credits: Cover, pp. 1, 3–32 (background) Lukas Rs/Shutterstock.com; Cover, sireonio/Shutterstock.com; Cover, Maksim Kabakou/Shutterstock.com; p. 5 Uber Images/Shutterstock.com; p. 7 © iStockphoto.com/4x6; p. 9 Jaroslava Nyvltova/Shutterstock.com; p. 11 ra2studio/Shutterstock.com; p. 13 Rawpixel.com/Shutterstock.com; p. 14 https://en.wikipedia.org/wiki/File:Steve_Wozniak_2012.jpg; p. 15 Twinsterphoto/Shutterstock.com; p. 17 Mint/Hindustan Times/Getty Images; pp. 19, 25 Bloomberg/Bloomberg/Getty Images; p. 21© iStockphoto.com/izusek; p. 23 F.Schmidt/Shutterstock.com; p. 27 Dragon Images/Shutterstock.com; p. 29 PAUL J. RICHARDS/AFP/Getty Images.

Library of Congress Cataloging-in-Publication Data

Names: Faust, Daniel R., author.
Title: Cybersecurity expert / Daniel R. Faust.
Description: New York : PowerKids Press, [2018] | Series: Behind the scenes with coders | Includes index.
Identifiers: LCCN 2016056434| ISBN 9781508155775 (pbk. book) | ISBN 9781508155591 (6 pack) | ISBN 9781508155713 (library bound book)
Subjects: LCSH: Computer security–Juvenile literature. | Computer security–Vocational guidance–Juvenile literature. | Computer crimes–Prevention–Juvenile literature. | Computer networks–Security measures–Juvenile literature.
Classification: LCC QA76.9.A25 F385 2018 | DDC 005.8–dc23
LC record available at https://lccn.loc.gov/2016056434

Manufactured in the United States of America

CPSIA Compliance Information: Batch #BS17PK: For Further Information contact Rosen Publishing, New York, New York at 1-800-237-9932

Contents

Staying Safe Online

Whether you're doing homework, playing games, or talking to your friends, you probably spend a lot of time online. Computers, smartphones, and tablets make it easy to **access** the Internet from just about anywhere. It's probably not surprising to learn that the average American between the ages of 7 and 16 spends about three hours a day on the Internet.

Although the Internet can be fun, it's important to remember that it can also be unsafe. People enter personal data such as birthdates, Social Security numbers, and financial information into a variety of different websites every day. Most of the time these websites are perfectly secure, but sometimes criminals can access a website and steal this data. Making sure websites and the data they contain remain safe and secure is the job of cybersecurity experts.

We spend more of our time online each year. It's important to remember that the more time we spend on the Internet, the more we expose ourselves to cybercriminals.

What Is Cybersecurity?

Cybersecurity is a branch of computer science that deals with protecting information systems from damage or theft. Cybersecurity experts are responsible for protecting the **hardware** and **software** of computers and computer **networks**, as well as the information stored on them. Cybersecurity experts are also responsible for protecting computer networks from **disruption** or misdirection of services.

Cybersecurity experts create countermeasures. Countermeasures are actions, devices, or methods that prevent or eliminate a threat. Countermeasures can be used to protect both software and hardware. Software can be designed from the ground up with security as a main feature. This kind of software will usually include a system that tracks user activity, allowing security experts to follow a cybercriminal's trail once an attack has been detected.

Cybersecurity involves more than just making sure there are no suspicious programs running on a computer network. Individual computers, including **servers**, need to be inspected and secured as well.

Firewalls are the most common form of network security. They can be software based or hardware based. Firewalls are used to filter or block data being sent between two or more computer networks. Firewalls prevent viruses and other threats from **infecting** a computer that is connected to the Internet or another outside network.

Physical countermeasures are built directly into the computer itself. Some computers have intrusion, or break-in, detection systems. These are special devices or software that know when a computer's case is opened. This can alert security experts that a computer has been **tampered** with. Another way to physically secure a computer is by disabling USB ports. This prevents unauthorized access to the computer and prevents someone from connecting an infected device to a secure computer.

Tech Talk ● ● ●

One way to protect digital data is through encryption. Encryption translates the data into a form that can't be read unless you have the correct password.

Terms of the Trade ▁ ⧉ X

Every career has its own vocabulary, or key terms. Here are some important words to know if you want to work in cybersecurity.

back door: A secret way of getting around a computer's security system.

bot: Software that runs programmed tasks over the Internet.

bug: A flaw in a computer program.

honeypot: A security countermeasure that uses seemingly valuable data to lure and trap cybercriminals.

malware: Any form of hostile or intrusive software, including viruses or worms.

worm: A type of malware that copies itself in order to infect other computers.

USB ports allow computer users to connect many kinds of devices to a computer. Some of these devices provide a handy way to store data, but they can also be used by criminals as a way to trick people into loading viruses or other harmful programs onto their computer.

Hacking, Phishing, Spoofing, and Clickjacking

Cybersecurity experts are concerned with a system's vulnerabilities, or weaknesses. One of their most important tasks is to secure systems against **exploitable** vulnerabilities. An exploitable vulnerability is a security flaw for which at least one working attack exists. These attacks are known as "exploits." Cyberattacks can occur for a number of different reasons. Some attackers are thrill seekers.

Hacktivists ▬ ⧉ X

While some criminals use hacking for financial gain, some hackers use it to promote a political agenda, or plan. These hackers are known as hacktivists, which is a combination of the words "hacker" and "**activist**." Some hacktivists feel it's their job to obtain and release information about social, economic, and political issues that those in power may not want the public to have access to. Perhaps the most famous hacktivist group is Anonymous.

The image of the computer hacker as a shadowy loner living in a dark, cramped apartment is far from the truth. Many hackers are friendly and outgoing. There are even annual hacker conventions, or gatherings, such as DEF CON.

Some are criminals looking for financial gain. Others are activists in search of evidence that could get people in trouble.

Most people are familiar with the term "hacker." The popular meaning of the word "hacker" is someone who breaks into computer systems for criminal purposes. In the computer community, a hacker is anyone who is a highly skilled computer expert. Among members of this community, a hacker who performs illegal break-ins is known as a "cracker."

Whatever you call them, cybercriminals frequently use the same kinds of attacks. It's the cybersecurity expert's job to become familiar with these attacks. A common kind of attack is the Trojan horse. A Trojan horse is a malicious, or very harmful, program that appears to be harmless. This tricks the user into **downloading** and running the program.

Spoofing and phishing are both ways for criminals to obtain sensitive information such as usernames, passwords, and credit card information. Both of these methods trick users by making a request for information look like it's from a safe source that the victim recognizes. Clickjacking hides viruses and other malware beneath clickable content on trusted websites. When a user clicks on this content, they unknowingly download a harmful program.

Tech Talk ● ● ●

Another common cyberattack is a distributed denial of service attack, or DDoS. Hackers use an army of bots to overwhelm a website's servers, making it impossible for others to access the site.

One of the most common cyberattacks targeting regular individuals is e-mail phishing. Hackers send an e-mail that looks like it came from a bank, credit card company, or other business, asking for the individual's personal information.

White Hats vs. Black Hats

In old Western movies, it was common for the good guys to wear white hats and the bad guys to wear black hats. These visual aids allowed viewers to identify the heroes and villains on sight. Over time, "white hat" and "black hat" have become standard terms for good guys and bad guys.

Woz ▬ ❐ X

Stephen Wozniak, nicknamed Woz, is the cofounder of Apple. While studying at the University of California, Woz discovered a way to bypass, or get around, the phone system. This is known as phone phreaking. He made devices called "blue boxes" and gave them to his friends. The blue boxes allowed Woz and his friends to make free long-distance phone calls. Wozniak became known as "Berkeley Blue" in the phone-phreak community.

Some people consider the hackers who make up the Anonymous collective "gray-hat hackers." They may be breaking the law by illegally hacking into computer networks, but they feel as though they're doing it for a good cause.

When it comes to cybersecurity, there are white-hat hackers and black-hat hackers. White-hat hackers are hackers who specialize in testing a computer network's vulnerabilities through the usual kinds of attacks used by criminal hackers, or black-hat hackers. Sometimes a company will employ two groups of white-hat hackers. One group, the red team, will attack a system. The other group, the blue team, will be responsible for defending the system.

Biggest Breach

The number of large data breaches, or break-ins, increases every year. Private corporations, **academic** and financial institutions, and governments have all been victims of cyberattacks. Each new hack reveals an exploit that cybersecurity experts have to deal with.

One of the largest data breaches to date was also one of the earliest. Between 2005 and 2012, a group of Russian and Ukrainian hackers attacked a number of banks and corporations, including JetBlue, 7-Eleven, and JCPenney. The hackers ended up stealing 160 million credit and debit card numbers and breached 800,000 bank accounts. In 2014, JPMorgan Chase and Co., the largest bank in the United States, was the victim of a cyberattack that exposed the data of more than half of all households in the country.

Some cybercriminals can steal your personal information using data skimmers. Data skimmers are devices that can be attached to ATMs and other card readers to record your data when you use an otherwise normal-looking machine.

Cybercriminals like to attack large companies such as Walmart and Amazon. Companies like this are the perfect targets for someone looking to steal the personal and financial data of millions of people at once.

In the last few years, some of the largest companies in the world have been victims of cyberattacks and data breaches. In 2014, eBay announced they had been hacked. The names, addresses, and passwords of around 145 million users had been exposed. Fortunately, eBay kept financial information on a different server, preventing the hackers from accessing this data. In December 2016, Yahoo announced that more than 1 billion user accounts had been hacked three years earlier. It can take a long time for companies to realize they've been hacked.

Target, Home Depot, and eBay have all been targeted by cybercriminals since 2013. The Target and Home Depot attacks resulted in the exposure of millions of debit and credit card numbers.

Not Just Fun and Games ▬ ⧉ X

In 2011, Sony's PlayStation Network (PSN) was the victim of a cyberattack. After discovering the breach, Sony shut down the gaming network for three weeks. In the end, the hackers were able to steal the personal and financial data of 77 million users. Three years later, in December 2014, Sony's PSN was the victim of another cyberattack. This time it was a DDoS attack that prevented users from accessing the network for several days.

Safer Systems and Stronger Codes

Sometimes it seems as though hackers and other cybercriminals are unstoppable. In reality, they're just intelligent individuals who are devoted to breaking the law. If you are a cybersecurity expert who is equally intelligent and devoted, you will rise to the challenge of stopping them.

No system can be completely secure. Any countermeasure that a cybersecurity expert designs will eventually be cracked. That's why cybersecurity

Add Extra Security — ▢ X

Two-step verification adds an extra layer of security by requiring a user to verify, or prove, who they are two times before entering a system. A user usually needs to enter a password and then another piece of information that is sent to a secondary device. This is often a text message sent to a personal phone. Setting up two-step verification is one of the easiest ways for a cybersecurity expert to make sure a computer network remains secure.

Two-step verification is one of the best ways to protect your personal information from getting stolen. Even if a hacker manages to crack your password, they would still need your phone to receive the secondary password.

experts must constantly work on building safer systems and writing stronger codes. One of the easiest ways to make sure a system remains secure is to be sure the software is up-to-date. Cybersecurity also relies on user education. Teaching people how to safely operate computer systems and avoid obvious security risks will make a cybersecurity expert's job much easier.

A New Kind of Warfare

A newer development in international conflicts is cyberwarfare. Cyberwarfare is when representatives of one nation hack into another nation's computer networks in order to cause damage or disruption. It's becoming more and more common.

One country may launch a cyberattack on another country for a number of reasons. Countries can use cyberattacks as a way to spy on each other. Hackers can break into a secure network and steal important documents or military secrets. It's believed that powerful countries are always spying on each other. A larger threat comes from the possibility of using a cyberattack for the purposes of **sabotage**. It would be very bad if a foreign country were able to damage the computers that control our country's power or water supplies or our telecommunications or transportation systems.

Many people see drones as the height of high-tech warfare. However, as advanced as unmanned drones might be, modern cyberwarfare has turned science fiction into scientific fact.

As cyberwarfare grows more common, cybersecurity experts are becoming an increasingly important part of national defense. Within just the first few months of 2016, there were four major cyberattacks on government organizations in the United States. Included in these attacks were NASA, the IRS, and the FBI. Cybersecurity experts have the important job of securing our nation's computer networks today. They also work hard to defend these networks from future cyberattacks.

Cybersecurity experts also study the defenses of the networks used by other countries. Countries such as Russia, China, and North Korea use a network of hackers to launch their cyberattacks. This means that having a strong defense may be the only way to truly protect our country's data.

Tech Talk ● ● ●

In 2015, a department of the U.S. government was hacked. Up to 14 million current and former federal employees had their private information exposed. The U.S. government was subject to about 61,000 cybersecurity breaches in 2014, which is proof that no system is truly safe.

Server rooms like this one are used to store digital data. Like banks and corporations, governments also store their sensitive information on servers. Making sure these servers are secure will prevent this information from getting into the wrong hands.

Skills You'll Need

Do you think a job in cybersecurity might be right for you? You'll need certain skills to be successful in this field. First, you'll need strong math and computer skills. Understanding the basics of operating systems such as Windows, UNIX, and Linux is key. Understanding programming languages, such as C++ and Java, is also important. You should also have excellent writing and communication skills.

Success in cybersecurity also requires certain personality traits. You should be able to work on your own as well as on a team. You may need to respond to stressful situations at all hours of the day and night. Problem solving, creative thinking, and attention to detail are important. You'll need to continue studying in order to stay informed about the latest software and potential exploits.

Many cybersecurity experts spend long hours sitting in front of a computer screen. If this sounds boring, cybersecurity may not be the best career for you.

Now Hiring

Imagine you've just graduated college with a degree in computer science and are starting to look for a job. Or maybe you're still in school and interested in finding an **internship**. Lucky for you, computers have become so common in the modern world that you can find a cybersecurity job in almost any industry.

Large corporations and financial institutions are preferred targets for cybercriminals and may need your help. Power supply companies, telecommunications systems, and transportation systems all rely on computers to function properly. This means they're open to cyberattacks and in need of security experts. You could also get a job at a private cybersecurity company. If you're interested in serving your country, the military and government agencies such as the NSA require intelligent and devoted individuals to protect important data.

Government agencies and the military handle sensitive data on a daily basis. Cybersecurity experts working for these organizations are serving their country and may also be saving lives.

The Future of Cybersecurity

As we rely more and more on the digital world to store important information, we also have to accept the fact that our data is at risk. Hackers and other cybercriminals may be extremely intelligent. Many are able to respond to new security countermeasures almost as soon as they're in place. In fact, it almost seems as though cybercriminals are capable of turning all of our digital devices against us.

The need for intelligent and hardworking people in the cybersecurity field will continue to grow. By increasing spending on cybersecurity efforts and making sure cybersecurity becomes something that is taught to children in school, we can make sure that our personal data is as safe and secure as possible.

Glossary

academic: Connected with a school, especially a college or university.

access: The ability to use or enter something.

activist: Someone who acts strongly in support of or against an issue.

disruption: The act of throwing something into disorder or interrupting it.

download: To copy data from one computer to another, often over the Internet.

exploitable: Capable of being used for someone's advantage or profit.

hardware: The physical parts of a computer system, such as wires, hard drives, keyboards, and monitors.

infect: To transmit or copy a virus from one computer to another.

internship: A job done, often without pay, in order to gain experience for a career.

network: A system of computers and databases that are all connected.

sabotage: Any act or process performed with the intent to damage or harm a business, government, or nation.

server: A computer or group of computers used by organizations for storing, processing, and distributing large amounts of data.

software: Programs that run on computers and perform certain functions.

tamper: To alter for an improper purpose or in an improper way.

Index

Websites

Due to the changing nature of Internet links, PowerKids Press has
developed an online list of websites related to the subject of this book.
This site is updated regularly. Please use this link to access the list:
www.powerkidslinks.com/bsc/cse